HYMNS
in Large Print

Published by

Augsburg Publishing House, Minneapolis

and

Board of Publication,

Lutheran Church in America, Philadelphia

ACKNOWLEDGMENTS

Ah, Holy Jesus
From the **Yattendon Hymnal** by permission of Oxford University Press.

O Sacred Head, Now Wounded
Copyright 1941 Concordia Publishing House, st. 4.
Used by permission.

A Mighty Fortress Is Our God
Copyright 1978 **Lutheran Book of Worship.**

Now the Silence
Copyright Jaroslav J. Vajda. Used by permission.

God Himself Is Present
Copyright Augsburg Publishing House, sts. 3-4.

Joyful, Joyful We Adore Thee
Reprinted by permission of Charles Scribner's Sons
from **The Poems of Henry Van Dyke** by Henry Van Dyke.

Built on a Rock
Copyright 1958 **Service Book and Hymnal.**

Lift High the Cross
By permission of Hymns Ancient and Modern, Ltd.

Praise and Thanksgiving
Copyright Albert F. Bayly. Used by permission.

Children of the Heavenly Father
Copyright Board of Publication, Lutheran Church in America.

Joy to the World 1

1 Joy to the world, the Lord is come!
  Let earth receive its King;
Let ev'ry heart prepare him room
  And heav'n and nature sing,
  And heav'n and nature sing,
And heav'n, and heav'n and nature sing.

2 Joy to the earth, the Savior reigns!
  Let all their songs employ,
While fields and floods, rocks, hills, and plains
  Repeat the sounding joy,
  Repeat the sounding joy,
Repeat, repeat the sounding joy.

3 No more let sin and sorrow grow
  Nor thorns infest the ground;
He comes to make his blessings flow
  Far as the curse is found,
  Far as the curse is found,
Far as, far as the curse is found.

4 He rules the world with truth and grace
  And makes the nations prove
The glories of his righteousness
  And wonders of his love,
  And wonders of his love,
And wonders, wonders of his love.

Isaac Watts, 1674-1748   (LBW 39)

2　Oh, Come, Oh, Come, Emmanuel

1 Oh, come, oh, come, Emmanuel,
And ransom captive Israel,
That mourns in lonely exile here
Until the Son of God appear.
Rejoice! Rejoice! Emmanuel
Shall come to you, O Israel.

2 Oh, come, oh, come, great Lord of might,
Who to your tribes on Sinai's height
In ancient times once gave the law
In cloud, and majesty, and awe.
Rejoice! Rejoice! Emmanuel
Shall come to you, O Israel.

3 Oh, come, strong Branch of Jesse, free
Your own from Satan's tyranny;
From depths of hell your people save
And give them vict'ry o'er the grave.
Rejoice! Rejoice! Emmanuel
Shall come to you, O Israel.

4 Oh, come, blest Dayspring, come and cheer
Our spirits by your advent here;
Disperse the gloomy clouds of night,
And death's dark shadows put to flight.
Rejoice! Rejoice! Emmanuel
Shall come to you, O Israel.

5 Oh, come, O Key of David, come,
   And open wide our heav'nly home;
   Make safe the way that leads on high,
   And close the path to misery.
   Rejoice! Rejoice! Emmanuel
   Shall come to you, O Israel.

Psalteriolum Cantionum Catholicarum, Köln, 1710;   (LBW 34)
tr. John M. Neale, 1818-1866, alt.

Silent Night, Holy Night!   3

1 Silent night, holy night!
   All is calm, all is bright
   Round yon virgin mother and child.
   Holy Infant, so tender and mild,
   Sleep in heavenly peace,
   Sleep in heavenly peace.

2 Silent night, holy night!
   Shepherds quake at the sight;
   Glories stream from heaven afar,
   Heav'nly hosts sing, Alleluia!
   Christ, the Savior, is born!
   Christ, the Savior, is born!

3 Silent night, holy night!
   Son of God, love's pure light
   Radiant beams from your holy face,
   With the dawn of redeeming grace,
   Jesus, Lord, at your birth,
   Jesus, Lord, at your birth.

Joseph Mohr, 1792-1849; tr. John F. Young, 1820-1885   (LBW 65)

Oh, Come, All Ye Faithful

1 Oh, come, all ye faithful,
Joyful and triumphant!
Oh, come ye, oh, come ye to Bethlehem;
Come and behold him
Born the king of angels:
Oh, come, let us adore him,
Oh, come, let us adore him,
Oh, come, let us adore him,
Christ the Lord!

2 The highest, most holy,
Light of light eternal,
Born of a virgin, a mortal he comes;
Son of the Father
Now in flesh appearing!
Oh, come, let us adore him,
Oh, come, let us adore him,
Oh, come, let us adore him,
Christ the Lord!

3 Sing, choirs of angels,
Sing in exultation,
Sing, all ye citizens of heaven above!
Glory to God
In the highest:
Oh, come, let us adore him,
Oh, come, let us adore him,
Oh, come, let us adore him,
Christ the Lord!

4 Yea, Lord, we greet thee,
  Born this happy morning;
  Jesus, to thee be glory giv'n!
  Word of the Father,
  Now in flesh appearing:
  Oh, come, let us adore him,
  Oh, come, let us adore him,
  Oh, come, let us adore him,
  Christ the Lord!

attr. John F. Wade, c. 1711-1786; tr. composite   (LBW 45)

Away in a Manger   5

1 Away in a manger, no crib for his bed,
  The little Lord Jesus laid down his sweet head;
  The stars in the sky looked down where he lay,
  The little Lord Jesus asleep on the hay.

2 The cattle were lowing; the poor baby wakes,
  But little Lord Jesus no crying he makes.
  I love you, Lord Jesus; look down from the sky
  And stay by my cradle till morning is nigh.

3 Be near me, Lord Jesus; I ask you to stay
  Close by me forever and love me, I pray.
  Bless all the dear children in your tender care
  And fit us for heaven to live with you there.

American, 1885   (LBW 67)

It Came upon the Midnight Clear

1 It came upon the midnight clear,
   That glorious song of old,
From angels bending near the earth
   To touch their harps of gold:
"Peace on the earth, good will to all,
   From heav'n's all-gracious king."
The world in solemn stillness lay
   To hear the angels sing.

2 Still through the cloven skies they come
   With peaceful wings unfurled,
And still their heav'nly music floats
   O'er all the weary world.
Above its sad and lowly plains
   They bend on hov'ring wing,
And ever o'er its babel sounds
   The blessèd angels sing.

3 And you, beneath life's crushing load,
   Whose forms are bending low,
Who toil along the climbing way
   With painful steps and slow:
Look now, for glad and golden hours
   Come swiftly on the wing;
Oh, rest beside the weary road
   And hear the angels sing!

4 For lo! The days are hast'ning on,
    By prophets seen of old,
  When with the ever-circling years
    Shall come the time foretold,
  When peace shall over all the earth
    Its ancient splendors fling,
  And all the world give back the song
    Which now the angels sing.

Edmund H. Sears, 1810-1876, alt.   (LBW 54)

Almighty God, you made this holy night shine with
the brightness of the true Light. Grant that here on
earth we may walk in the light of Jesus' presence
and in the last day wake to the brightness of his
glory; through your only Son, Jesus Christ our Lord,
who lives and reigns with you and the Holy Spirit,
one God, now and forever. Amen

O Little Town of Bethlehem

1 O little town of Bethlehem,
  How still we see thee lie!
Above thy deep and dreamless sleep
  The silent stars go by;
Yet in thy dark streets shineth
  The everlasting light.
The hopes and fears of all the years
  Are met in thee tonight.

2 For Christ is born of Mary,
  And, gathered all above
While mortals sleep, the angels keep
  Their watch of wond'ring love.
O morning stars, together
  Proclaim the holy birth,
And praises sing to God the king,
  And peace to all the earth!

3 How silently, how silently
  The wondrous gift is giv'n!
So God imparts to human hearts
  The blessings of his heav'n.
No ear may hear his coming;
  But, in this world of sin,
Where meek souls will receive him, still
  The dear Christ enters in.

4 **O holy Child of Bethlehem,**
      Descend to us, we pray;
   Cast out our sin, and enter in,
      Be born in us today.
   We hear the Christmas angels
      The great glad tidings tell;
   Oh, come to us, abide with us,
      Our Lord Immanuel!

Phillips Brooks, 1835-1893   (LBW 41)

Almighty God, you wonderfully created and yet more wonderfully restored the dignity of human nature. In your mercy, let us share the divine life of Jesus Christ who came to share our humanity, and who now lives and reigns with you and the Holy Spirit, one God, now and forever. Amen

      # Hark! The Herald Angels Sing

1 Hark! The herald angels sing,
"Glory to the newborn king;
Peace on earth, and mercy mild,
God and sinners reconciled."
Joyful, all you nations, rise;
Join the triumph of the skies;
With angelic hosts proclaim,
"Christ is born in Bethlehem!"
Hark! The herald angels sing,
"Glory to the newborn king!"

2 Christ, by highest heav'n adored,
Christ, the everlasting Lord,
Late in time behold him come,
Offspring of a virgin's womb.
Veiled in flesh the Godhead see!
Hail, incarnate deity!
Pleased as man with us to dwell,
Jesus, our Emmanuel!
Hark! The herald angels sing,
"Glory to the newborn king!"

3 Hail the heav'n-born Prince of Peace!
Hail the sun of righteousness!
Light and life to all he brings,
Ris'n with healing in his wings.
Mild he lays his glory by,
Born that we no more may die,

Born to raise each child of earth,
Born to give us second birth.
Hark! The herald angels sing,
"Glory to the newborn king!"

Charles Wesley, 1707-1788, alt. (LBW 60)

Brightest and Best of the Stars 9

1 Brightest and best of the stars of the morning,
   Dawn on our darkness and lend us your aid.
Star of the East, the horizon adorning,
   Guide where our infant Redeemer is laid.

2 Cold on his cradle the dewdrops are shining;
   Low lies his head with the beasts of the stall;
Angels adore him in slumber reclining,
   Maker and Monarch and Savior of all.

3 Shall we not yield him, in costly devotion,
   Fragrance of Edom and off'rings divine,
Gems of the mountain and pearls of the ocean,
   Myrrh from the forest or gold from the mine?

4 Vainly we offer each ample oblation,
   Vainly with gifts would his favor secure;
Richer by far is the heart's adoration,
   Dearer to God are the prayers of the poor.

5 Brightest and best of the stars of the morning,
   Dawn on our darkness and lend us your aid.
Star of the East, the horizon adorning,
   Guide where our infant Redeemer is laid.

Reginald Heber, 1783-1826, alt. (LBW 84)

10   As with Gladness Men of Old

1 As with gladness men of old
  Did the guiding star behold;
  As with joy they hailed its light,
  Leading onward, beaming bright;
  So, most gracious Lord, may we
  Evermore be led by thee.

2 As with joyful steps they sped,
  Savior, to thy lowly bed,
  There to bend the knee before
  Thee, whom heav'n and earth adore;
  So may we with willing feet
  Ever seek thy mercy seat.

3 As they offered gifts most rare
  At thy cradle, rude and bare,
  So may we with holy joy,
  Pure and free from sin's alloy,
  All our costliest treasures bring,
  Christ, to thee, our heav'nly king.

4 Holy Jesus, ev'ry day
  Keep us in the narrow way;
  And when earthly things are past,
  Bring our ransomed souls at last
  Where they need no star to guide,
  Where no clouds thy glory hide.

5 In the heav'nly country bright
   Need they no created light;
   Thou its light, its joy, its crown,
   Thou its sun which goes not down;
   There forever may we sing
   Alleluias to our King.

William C. Dix, 1837-1898, alt.   (LBW 82)

Lord God, on this day you revealed your Son to the nations by the leading of a star. Lead us now by faith to know your presence in our lives, and bring us at last to the full vision of your glory, through your Son, Jesus Christ our Lord, who lives and reigns with you and the Holy Spirit, one God, now and forever. Amen

1 Were you there when they crucified my Lord?
  Were you there when they crucified my Lord?
  Oh, sometimes it causes me to tremble,
    tremble, tremble.
  Were you there when they crucified my Lord?

2 Were you there when they nailed him to the tree?
  Were you there when they nailed him to the tree?
  Oh, sometimes it causes me to tremble,
    tremble, tremble.
  Were you there when they nailed him to the tree?

3 Were you there when they laid him in the tomb?
  Were you there when they laid him in the tomb?
  Oh, sometimes it causes me to tremble,
    tremble, tremble.
  Were you there when they laid him in the tomb?

4 Were you there when God raised him from
    the tomb?
  Were you there when God raised him from
    the tomb?
  Oh, sometimes it causes me to tremble,
    tremble, tremble.
  Were you there when God raised him from
    the tomb?

Negro spiritual, alt.   (LBW 92)

Beneath the Cross of Jesus 12

1 Beneath the cross of Jesus
  I long to take my stand;
The shadow of a mighty rock
  Within a weary land,
A home within a wilderness,
  A rest upon the way,
From the burning of the noontide heat
  And burdens of the day.

2 Upon the cross of Jesus,
  My eye at times can see
The very dying form of one
  Who suffered there for me.
And from my contrite heart, with tears,
  Two wonders I confess:
The wonder of his glorious love
  And my unworthiness.

3 I take, O cross, your shadow
  For my abiding place;
I ask no other sunshine than
  The sunshine of his face;
Content to let the world go by,
  To know no gain nor loss,
My sinful self my only shame,
  My glory all, the cross.

Elizabeth C. Clephane, 1830-1869   (LBW 107)

13   In the Cross of Christ I Glory

1 In the cross of Christ I glory,
    Tow'ring o'er the wrecks of time.
All the light of sacred story
    Gathers round its head sublime.

2 When the woes of life o'ertake me,
    Hopes deceive, and fears annoy,
Never shall the cross forsake me;
    Lo, it glows with peace and joy.

3 When the sun of bliss is beaming
    Light and love upon my way,
From the cross the radiance streaming
    Adds more luster to the day.

4 Bane and blessing, pain and pleasure,
    By the cross are sanctified;
Peace is there that knows no measure,
    Joys that through all time abide.

John Bowring, 1792-1872   (LBW 104)

14   O Sacred Head, Now Wounded

1 O sacred head, now wounded,
    With grief and shame weighed down,
Now scornfully surrounded
    With thorns, thine only crown;
O sacred head, what glory,
    What bliss till now was thine!
Yet, though despised and gory,
    I joy to call thee mine.

2 How art thou pale with anguish,
    With sore abuse and scorn;
How does that visage languish
    Which once was bright as morn!
Thy grief and bitter Passion
    Were all for sinners' gain;
Mine, mine was the transgression,
    But thine the deadly pain.

3 What language shall I borrow
    To thank thee, dearest friend,
For this thy dying sorrow,
    Thy pity without end?
Oh, make me thine forever,
    And, should I fainting be,
Lord, let me never, never
    Outlive my love to thee.

4 Lord, be my consolation;
    Shield me when I must die;
Remind me of thy Passion
    When my last hour draws nigh.
These eyes, new faith receiving,
    From thee shall never move;
For he who dies believing
    Dies safely in thy love.

(LBW 116)

Go to Dark Gethsemane

1 Go to dark Gethsemane,
All who feel the tempter's pow'r;
Your Redeemer's conflict see.
Watch with him one bitter hour;
Turn not from his griefs away;
Learn from Jesus Christ to pray.

2 Follow to the judgment hall,
View the Lord of life arraigned;
Oh, the wormwood and the gall!
Oh, the pangs his soul sustained!
Shun not suff'ring, shame, or loss;
Learn from him to bear the cross.

3 Calv'ry's mournful mountain climb;
There, adoring at his feet,
Mark that miracle of time,
God's own sacrifice complete.
"It is finished!" hear him cry;
Learn from Jesus Christ to die.

4 Early hasten to the tomb
Where they laid his breathless clay;
All is solitude and gloom.
Who has taken him away?
Christ is ris'n! He meets our eyes.
Savior, teach us so to rise.

James Montgomery, 1771-1854 (LBW 109)

Ah, Holy Jesus 16

1 Ah, holy Jesus, how hast thou offended
That man to judge thee hath in hate pretended?
By foes derided, by thine own rejected,
   O most afflicted.

2 Who was the guilty? Who brought this upon thee?
Alas, my treason, Jesus, hath undone thee.
'Twas I, Lord Jesus, I it was denied thee;
   I crucified thee.

3 Lo, the Good Shepherd for the sheep is offered;
The slave hath sinnèd, and the Son hath suffered;
For man's atonement, while he nothing heedeth,
   God intercedeth.

4 For me, kind Jesus, was thine incarnation,
Thy mortal sorrow, and thy life's oblation;
Thy death of anguish and thy bitter Passion,
   For my salvation.

5 Therefore, kind Jesus, since I cannot pay thee,
I do adore thee, and will ever pray thee;
Think on thy pity and thy love unswerving,
   Not my deserving.

© Johann Heermann, 1585-1647;
tr. Robert Bridges, 1844-1930, alt.

(LBW 123)

Christ Is Risen! Alleluia!

1 Christ is risen! Alleluia!
   Risen our victorious head!
Sing his praises! Alleluia!
   Christ is risen from the dead!
Gratefully our hearts adore him
   As his light once more appears;
Bowing down in joy before him,
   Rising up from griefs and tears.
Christ is risen! Alleluia!
   Risen our victorious head!
Sing his praises! Alleluia!
   Christ is risen from the dead!

2 Christ is risen! All the sadness
   Of our Lenten fast is o'er;
Through the open gates of gladness
   He returns to life once more;
Death and hell before him bending
   See him rise, the victor now,
Angels on his steps attending,
   Glory round his wounded brow.
Christ is risen! Alleluia!
   Risen our victorious head!
Sing his praises! Alleluia!
   Christ is risen from the dead!

3 Christ is risen! All the sorrow
    That last evening round him lay
Now has found a glorious morrow
    In the rising of today.
See the grave its first-fruits giving,
    Springing up from holy ground;
He was dead, but now is living;
    He was lost, but he is found.
Christ is risen! Alleluia!
    Risen our victorious head!
Sing his praises! Alleluia!
    Christ is risen from the dead!

4 Christ is risen! Henceforth never
    Death or hell shall us enthrall;
Be we Christ's, in him forever
    We have triumphed over all.
All the doubting and dejection
    Of our trembling hearts have ceased;
Hail the day of resurrection!
    Let us rise and keep the feast.
Christ is risen! Alleluia!
    Risen our victorious head!
Sing his praises! Alleluia!
    Christ is risen from the dead!

John S. B. Monsell, 1811-1875, alt.   (LBW 131)

18   Hallelujah! Jesus Lives!

1 Hallelujah! Jesus lives!
   He is now the Living One;
   From the gloomy halls of death
   Christ, the conqueror, has gone,
   Bright forerunner to the skies
   Of his people, yet to rise.

2 Jesus lives! Why do you weep?
   Why that sad and mournful sigh?
   He who died our brother here
   Lives our brother still on high,
   Lives forever to bestow
   Blessings on his Church below.

3 Jesus lives! And thus, my soul,
   Life eternal waits for you;
   Joined to him, your living head,
   Where he is, you shall be too;
   With the Lord, at his right hand,
   As a victor you shall stand.

4 Jesus lives! Let all rejoice.
   Praise him, ransomed of the earth.
   Praise him in a nobler song,
   Cherubim of heav'nly birth.
   Praise the victor king, whose sway
   Sin and death and hell obey.

5 Hallelujah! Angels, sing!
   Join with us in hymns of praise.
   Let your chorus swell the strain
   Which our feebler voices raise:
   Glory to our God above
   And on earth his peace and love!

Carl B. Garve, 1763-1841;   (LBW 147)
tr. Jane L. Borthwick, 1813-1897, alt.

Jesus Christ Is Risen Today   19

1 Jesus Christ is ris'n today, Alleluia!
   Our triumphant holy day, Alleluia!
   Who did once upon the cross, Alleluia!
   Suffer to redeem our loss. Alleluia!

2 Hymns of praise then let us sing, Alleluia!
   Unto Christ, our heav'nly king, Alleluia!
   Who endured the cross and grave, Alleluia!
   Sinners to redeem and save. Alleluia!

3 But the pains which he endured, Alleluia!
   Our salvation have procured; Alleluia!
   Now above the sky he's king, Alleluia!
   Where the angels ever sing. Alleluia!

4 Sing we to our God above, Alleluia!
   Praise eternal as his love; Alleluia!
   Praise him, all you heav'nly host, Alleluia!
   Father, Son, and Holy Ghost. Alleluia!

Latin carol, 14th cent., sts. 1-3; Charles Wesley,   (LBW 151)
1707-1788, st. 4; tr. Lyra Davidica, London, 1708, sts. 1-3

20   The Strife Is O'er, the Battle Done

Alleluia, alleluia, alleluia!

1 The strife is o'er, the battle done;
Now is the victor's triumph won!
Now be the song of praise begun.
   Alleluia!

2 The pow'rs of death have done their worst,
But Christ their legions has dispersed.
Let shouts of holy joy outburst.
   Alleluia!

3 The three sad days have quickly sped,
He rises glorious from the dead.
All glory to our risen head!
   Alleluia!

4 He broke the age-bound chains of hell;
The bars from heav'n's high portals fell.
Let hymns of praise his triumph tell.
   Alleluia!

5 Lord, by the stripes which wounded you,
From death's sting free your servants too,
That we may live and sing to you.
   Alleluia!

Alleluia, alleluia, alleluia!

Symphonia Sirenum, Köln, 1695;
tr. Francis Pott, 1832-1909

(LBW 135)

Holy, Holy, Holy 21

1 Holy, holy, holy, Lord God Almighty!
Early in the morning our song shall rise to thee.
Holy, holy, holy, merciful and mighty!
God in three Persons, blessèd Trinity!

2 Holy, holy, holy! All the saints adore thee,
Casting down their golden crowns around the
glassy sea;
Cherubim and seraphim falling down before thee,
Which wert and art and evermore shalt be.

3 Holy, holy, holy! Though the darkness hide thee,
Though the eye made blind by sin thy glory may
not see,
Only thou art holy; there is none beside thee,
Perfect in pow'r, in love and purity.

4 Holy, holy, holy! Lord God Almighty!
All thy works shall praise thy name in earth and
sky and sea.
Holy, holy, holy, merciful and mighty!
God in three Persons, blessèd Trinity!

Reginald Heber, 1783-1826, alt.   (LBW 165)

Crown Him with Many Crowns

1   Crown him with many crowns,
    The Lamb upon his throne;
Hark, how the heav'nly anthem drowns
    All music but its own.
    Awake, my soul, and sing
    Of him who died for thee,
And hail him as thy matchless king
    Through all eternity.

2   Crown him the virgin's Son,
    The God incarnate born,
Whose arm those crimson trophies won
    Which now his brow adorn;
    Fruit of the mystic rose,
    Yet of that rose the stem,
The root whence mercy ever flows,
    The babe of Bethlehem.

3   Crown him the Lord of love–
    Behold his hands and side,
Rich wounds, yet visible above,
    In beauty glorified.
    No angels in the sky
    Can fully bear that sight,
But downward bend their burning eyes
    At mysteries so bright.

4   Crown him the Lord of life,
    Who triumphed o'er the grave
And rose victorious in the strife
    For those he came to save.
    His glories now we sing,
    Who died and rose on high,
Who died, eternal life to bring,
    And lives that death may die.

5   Crown him the Lord of peace,
    Whose pow'r a scepter sways
From pole to pole, that wars may cease,
    Absorbed in prayer and praise.
    His reign shall know no end,
    And round his piercèd feet
Fair flow'rs of paradise extend
    Their fragrance ever sweet.

6   Crown him the Lord of years,
    The potentate of time,
Creator of the rolling spheres,
    Ineffably sublime.
    All hail, Redeemer, hail!
    For thou hast died for me;
Thy praise and glory shall not fail
    Throughout eternity.

Matthew Bridges, 1800-1894;   (LBW 170)
Godfrey Thring, 1823-1903

A Mighty Fortress Is Our God

1 A mighty fortress is our God,
   A sword and shield victorious;
He breaks the cruel oppressor's rod
   And wins salvation glorious.
   The old satanic foe
   Has sworn to work us woe!
   With craft and dreadful might
   He arms himself to fight.
On earth he has no equal.

2 No strength of ours can match his might!
   We would be lost, rejected.
But now a champion comes to fight.
   Whom God himself elected.
   You ask who this may be?
   The Lord of hosts is he!
   Christ Jesus, mighty Lord,
   God's only Son, adored.
He holds the field victorious.

3 Though hordes of devils fill the land
   All threat'ning to devour us,
We tremble not, unmoved we stand;
   They cannot overpow'r us.
   Let this world's tyrant rage;
   In battle we'll engage!
   His might is doomed to fail;
   God's judgment must prevail!
One little word subdues him.

4 God's Word forever shall abide,
    No thanks to foes, who fear it;
For God himself fights by our side
    With weapons of the Spirit.
    Were they to take our house,
    Goods, honor, child, or spouse,
    Though life be wrenched away,
    They cannot win the day.
The kingdom's ours forever!

© Martin Luther, 1483-1546; tr. hymnal version, 1978   (LBW 229)

Lord, Keep Us Steadfast   24

1 Lord, keep us steadfast in your Word;
    Curb those who by deceit or sword
    Would wrest the kingdom from your Son
    And bring to nought all he has done.

2 Lord Jesus Christ, your pow'r make known,
    For you are Lord of lords alone;
    Defend your holy Church, that we
    May sing your praise triumphantly.

3 O Comforter of priceless worth,
    Send peace and unity on earth;
    Support us in our final strife
    And lead us out of death to life.

Martin Luther, 1483-1546;   (LBW 230)
tr. Catherine Winkworth, 1829-1878, alt.

1 Break now the bread of life,
 Dear Lord, to me,
As once you broke the loaves
 Beside the sea.
Beyond the sacred page
 I seek you, Lord;
My spirit waits for you,
 O living Word.

2 Bless your own truth, dear Lord,
 To me, to me,
As when you blest the bread
 By Galilee.
Then shall all bondage cease,
 All fetters fall;
And I shall find my peace,
 My All-in-All!

3 You are the bread of life,
 O Lord, to me.
Your holy Word the truth
 That rescues me.
Give me to eat and live
 With you above;
Teach me to love your truth,
 For you are love.

4 Oh, send your Spirit, Lord,
    Now unto me,
That he may touch my eyes
    And make me see.
Show me the truth concealed
    Within your Word,
And in your book revealed
    I see my Lord.

Mary A. Lathbury, 1841-1913, alt.   (LBW 235)

Let Us Break Bread Together   26

1 Let us break bread together on our knees;
Let us break bread together on our knees.
    When I fall on my knees,
    With my face to the rising sun,
    O Lord, have mercy on me.

2 Let us drink wine together on our knees;
Let us drink wine together on our knees.
    When I fall on my knees,
    With my face to the rising sun,
    O Lord, have mercy on me.

3 Let us praise God together on our knees;
Let us praise God together on our knees.
    When I fall on my knees,
    With my face to the rising sun,
    O Lord, have mercy on me.

Negro spiritual   (LBW 212)

 # O Bread of Life from Heaven

1 O Bread of life from heaven,
　 O Food to pilgrims given,
　　 O Manna from above:
　 Feed with the blessed sweetness
　 Of your divine completeness
　 The souls that want and need your love.

2 O Fount of grace redeeming,
　 O River ever streaming
　　 From Jesus' wounded side:
　 Come now, your love bestowing
　 On thirsting souls, and flowing
　 Till all are fully satisfied.

3 We love you, Jesus, tender,
　 In all your hidden splendor
　　 Within these means of grace.
　 Oh, let the veil be riven,
　 And our clear eye in heaven
　 Behold your glory face to face.

© Latin hymn, c. 1661; tr. composite, alt.　　　　　(LBW 222)

Now the Silence 28

Now the silence,
Now the peace,
Now the empty hands uplifted;
Now the kneeling,
Now the plea,
Now the Father's arms in welcome;
Now the hearing,
Now the pow'r,
Now the vessel brimmed for pouring;
Now the body,
Now the blood,
Now the joyful celebration;
Now the wedding,
Now the songs,
Now the heart forgiven leaping;
Now the Spirit's visitation,
Now the Son's epiphany,
Now the Father's blessing.
Now. Now. Now.

© Jaroslav J. Vajda, b. 1919   (LBW 205)

 # God Himself Is Present

1 God himself is present;
   Let us now adore him
And with awe appear before him!
   God is in his temple;
   All within keep silence,
Prostrate lie with deepest rev'rence.
   Him alone God we own,
   Him, our God and Savior;
   Praise his name forever!

2 God himself is present;
   Hear the harps resounding;
See the hosts the throne surrounding!
   "Holy, holy, holy!"
   Hear the hymn ascending,
Songs of saints and angels blending.
   Bow your ear to us here:
   Hear, O Christ, the praises
   That your Church now raises.

3 Light of light eternal,
   All things penetrating,
For your rays our soul is waiting.
   As the tender flowers,
   Willingly unfolding,
To the sun their faces holding:
   Even so would we do,
   Light from you obtaining,
   Strength to serve you gaining.

4   Come, celestial Being,
     Make our hearts your dwelling,
   Ev'ry carnal thought dispelling.
     By your Holy Spirit
     Sanctify us truly,
   Teaching us to love you only.
     Where we go here below,
     Let us bow before you
     And in truth adore you.

© Gerhard Tersteegen, 1697-1769; tr. composite   (LBW 249)

O most loving Father, you want us to give thanks for all things, to fear nothing except losing you, and to lay all our cares on you, knowing that you care for us. Protect us from faithless fears and worldly anxieties, and grant that no clouds in this mortal life may hide from us the light of your immortal love shown to us in your Son, Jesus Christ our Lord. Amen

30   Open Now Thy Gates of Beauty

1 Open now thy gates of beauty,
   Zion, let me enter there,
Where my soul in joyful duty
   Waits for God who answers prayer.
   Oh, how blessèd is this place,
   Filled with solace, light, and grace!

2 Gracious God, I come before thee;
   Come thou also unto me;
Where we find thee and adore thee,
   There a heav'n on earth must be.
   To my heart, oh, enter thou,
   Let it be thy temple now!

3 Here thy praise is gladly chanted,
   Here thy seed is duly sown;
Let my soul, where it is planted,
   Bring forth precious sheaves alone,
   So that all I hear may be
   Fruitful unto life in me.

4 Thou my faith increase and quicken,
   Let me keep thy gift divine;
Howsoe'er temptations thicken,
   May thy Word still o'er me shine
   As my guiding star through life,
   As my comfort in all strife.

5 Speak, O God, and I will hear thee,
   Let thy will be done indeed;
 May I undisturbed draw near thee
   While thou dost thy people feed.
   Here of life the fountain flows;
   Here is balm for all our woes.

Benjamin Schmolck, 1672-1737;
tr. Catherine Winkworth, 1829-1878, alt.   (LBW 250)

Savior, Again to Your Dear Name 31

1 Savior, again to your dear name we raise
   With one accord our parting hymn of praise;
   Once more we bless you ere our worship cease,
   Then, lowly bending, wait your word of peace.

2 Grant us your peace upon our homeward way;
   With you began, with you shall end the day;
   Guard all the lips from sin, the hearts from shame,
   That in this house have called upon your name.

3 Grant us your peace, Lord, through the coming
      night;
   For us transform its darkness into light.
   Keep us from harm and danger till the dawn;
   Your evening presence promise to your own.

4 Grant us your peace throughout our earthly life,
   Our balm in sorrow, and our stay in strife;
   Then, when your voice shall bid our conflict cease,
   Call us, O Lord, to your eternal peace.

John Ellerton, 1826-1893, alt.   (LBW 262)

32   All People That on Earth Do Dwell

1 All people that on earth do dwell,
  Sing to the Lord with cheerful voice;
  Him serve with mirth, his praise forth tell;
  Come ye before him and rejoice.

2 Know that the Lord is God indeed;
  Without our aid he did us make.
  We are his folk, he doth us feed,
  And for his sheep he doth us take.

3 Oh, enter then his gates with praise;
  Approach with joy his courts unto;
  Praise, laud, and bless his name always,
  For it is seemly so to do.

4 For why? The Lord our God is good:
  His mercy is forever sure;
  His truth at all times firmly stood,
  And shall from age to age endure.

5 To Father, Son, and Holy Ghost,
  The God whom heav'n and earth adore,
  From us and from the angel host
  Be praise and glory evermore.

William Kethe, d. c. 1593   (LBW 245)

Lord, Dismiss Us with Your Blessing 33

1 Lord, dismiss us with your blessing,
   Fill our hearts with joy and peace;
Let us each, your love possessing,
   Triumph in redeeming grace.
Oh, refresh us; oh, refresh us,
   Trav'ling through this wilderness.

2 Thanks we give and adoration
   For your Gospel's joyful sound.
May the fruits of your salvation
   In our hearts and lives abound.
Ever faithful, ever faithful
   To your truth may we be found.

3 Savior, when your love shall call us
   From our struggling pilgrim way,
Let no fear of death appall us,
   Glad your summons to obey.
May we ever, may we ever
   Reign with you in endless day.

attr. John Fawcett, 1740-1817, sts. 1-2;
Godfrey Thring, 1823-1903, st. 3, alt.

(LBW 259)

34   Now the Day Is Over

1 Now the day is over;
   Night is drawing nigh;
Shadows of the evening
   Steal across the sky.

2 Jesus, give the weary
   Calm and sweet repose;
With your tend'rest blessing
   May our eyelids close.

3 Comfort ev'ry suff'rer
   Watching late in pain;
Those who plan some evil,
   From their sin restrain.

4 Through the long nightwatches
   May your angels spread
Their bright wings above me,
   Watching round my bed.

5 When the morning wakens,
   Then may I arise
Pure and fresh and sinless
   In your holy eyes.

6 Glory to the Father,
   Glory to the Son,
And to you, blest Spirit,
   While the ages run.

Sabine Baring-Gould, 1834-1924, alt.   (LBW 280)

Abide with Me {35}

1 Abide with me, fast falls the eventide.
The darkness deepens; Lord, with me abide.
When other helpers fail and comforts flee,
Help of the helpless, oh, abide with me.

2 I need thy presence ev'ry passing hour;
What but thy grace can foil the tempter's pow'r?
Who like thyself my guide and stay can be?
Through cloud and sunshine, oh, abide with me.

3 Swift to its close ebbs out life's little day;
Earth's joys grow dim, its glories pass away;
Change and decay in all around I see;
O thou who changest not, abide with me.

4 I fear no foe, with thee at hand to bless;
Ills have no weight, and tears no bitterness.
Where is death's sting? Where, grave, thy victory?
I triumph still, if thou abide with me!

5 Hold thou thy cross before my closing eyes,
Shine through the gloom, and point me to the
skies;
Heav'n's morning breaks, and earth's vain
shadows flee;
In life, in death, O Lord, abide with me.

Henry F. Lyte, 1793-1847   (LBW 272)

36   Love Divine, All Loves Excelling

1 Love divine, all loves excelling,
    Joy of heav'n, to earth come down!
Fix in us thy humble dwelling,
    All thy faithful mercies crown.
Jesus, thou art all compassion,
    Pure, unbounded love thou art;
Visit us with thy salvation,
    Enter ev'ry trembling heart.

2 Breathe, oh, breathe thy loving Spirit
    Into ev'ry troubled breast;
Let us all in thee inherit;
    Let us find thy promised rest.
Take away the love of sinning;
    Alpha and Omega be;
End of faith, as its beginning,
    Set our hearts at liberty.

3 Come, Almighty, to deliver;
    Let us all thy life receive;
Suddenly return, and never,
    Nevermore thy temples leave.
Thee we would be always blessing,
    Serve thee as thy hosts above,
Pray, and praise thee without ceasing,
    Glory in thy perfect love.

4 Finish then thy new creation,
    Pure and spotless let us be;
Let us see thy great salvation
    Perfectly restored in thee!

Changed from glory into glory,
   Till in heav'n we take our place,
Till we cast our crowns before thee,
   Lost in wonder, love, and praise!

Charles Wesley, 1707-1788   (LBW 315)

Jesus, Savior, Pilot Me   37

1 Jesus, Savior, pilot me
   Over life's tempestuous sea;
   Unknown waves before me roll,
   Hiding rock and treach'rous shoal;
   Chart and compass come from thee.
   Jesus, Savior, pilot me.

2 As a mother stills her child,
   Thou canst hush the ocean wild;
   Boist'rous waves obey thy will
   When thou say'st to them: "Be still."
   Wondrous sov'reign of the sea,
   Jesus, Savior, pilot me.

3 When at last I near the shore,
   And the fearful breakers roar
   Twixt me and the peaceful rest,
   Then, while leaning on thy breast,
   May I hear thee say to me:
   "Fear not, I will pilot thee."

Edward Hopper, 1818-1888   (LBW 334)

1 Mine eyes have seen the glory
        of the coming of the Lord;
He is trampling out the vintage
        where the grapes of wrath are stored;
He has loosed the fateful lightning
        of his terrible swift sword:
    His truth is marching on.
    Glory, glory! Hallelujah!
    Glory, glory! Hallelujah!
    Glory, glory! Hallelujah!
    His truth is marching on.

2 He has sounded forth the trumpet
        that shall never call retreat;
He is sifting out the hearts of men
        before his judgment seat.
Oh, be swift, my soul, to answer him;
        be jubilant, my feet!
    Our God is marching on.
    Glory, glory! Hallelujah!
    Glory, glory! Hallelujah!
    Glory, glory! Hallelujah!
    His truth is marching on.

3 In the beauty of the lilies
    Christ was born across the sea,
With a glory in his bosom
    that transfigures you and me.
As he died to make men holy,
    let us live to make men free,
While God is marching on.
Glory, glory! Hallelujah!
Glory, glory! Hallelujah!
Glory, glory! Hallelujah!
His truth is marching on.

Julia Ward Howe, 1819-1910   (LBW 332)

I love you, O Lord my strength,
    O Lord my stronghold,
    my crag, and my haven.
My God, my rock
in whom I put my trust,
    my shield, the horn of my salvation,
    and my refuge:
You are worthy of praise.

(Psalm 18:1-2)

39 Guide Me Ever, Great Redeemer

1 Guide me ever, great Redeemer,
    Pilgrim through this barren land.
I am weak, but you are mighty;
    Hold me with your pow'rful hand.
Bread of heaven, bread of heaven,
    Feed me now and evermore,
    Feed me now and evermore.

2 Open now the crystal fountain
    Where the healing waters flow;
Let the fire and cloudy pillar
    Lead me all my journey through.
Strong deliv'rer, strong deliv'rer,
    Shield me with your mighty arm,
    Shield me with your mighty arm.

3 When I tread the verge of Jordan,
    Bid my anxious fears subside;
Death of death and hell's destruction,
    Land me safe on Canaan's side.
Songs and praises, songs and praises,
    I will raise forevermore,
    I will raise forevermore.

William Williams, 1717-1791; tr. composite, alt.   (LBW 343)

O God, Our Help in Ages Past 40

1 O God, our help in ages past,
   Our hope for years to come,
Our shelter from the stormy blast,
   And our eternal home:

2 Under the shadow of your throne
   Your saints have dwelt secure;
Sufficient is your arm alone,
   And our defense is sure.

3 Before the hills in order stood
   Or earth received its frame,
From everlasting you are God,
   To endless years the same.

4 A thousand ages in your sight
   Are like an evening gone,
Short as the watch that ends the night
   Before the rising sun.

5 Time, like an ever-rolling stream,
   Soon bears us all away;
We fly forgotten, as a dream
   Dies at the op'ning day.

6 O God, our help in ages past,
   Our hope for years to come,
Still be our guard while troubles last
   And our eternal home!

Isaac Watts, 1674-1748, alt.   (LBW 320)

41 All Hail the Power of Jesus' Name

1 All hail the pow'r of Jesus' name!
    Let angels prostrate fall;
Bring forth the royal diadem
    And crown him Lord of all.
Bring forth the royal diadem
    And crown him Lord of all.

2 Crown him, you martyrs of our God,
    Who from his altar call;
Extol the stem of Jesse's rod
    And crown him Lord of all.
Extol the stem of Jesse's rod
    And crown him Lord of all.

3 O seed of Israel's chosen race
    Now ransomed from the fall,
Hail him who saves you by his grace
    And crown him Lord of all.
Hail him who saves you by his grace
    And crown him Lord of all.

4 Hail him, you heirs of David's line,
    Whom David Lord did call–
The God Incarnate, man divine–
    And crown him Lord of all.
The God Incarnate, man divine–
    And crown him Lord of all.

5 Sinners, whose love can ne'er forget
     The wormwood and the gall,
   Go, spread your trophies at his feet
     And crown him Lord of all.
   Go, spread your trophies at his feet
     And crown him Lord of all.

6 Let ev'ry kindred, ev'ry tribe
     On this terrestrial ball
   To him all majesty ascribe
     And crown him Lord of all.
   To him all majesty ascribe
     And crown him Lord of all.

7 Oh, that with yonder sacred throng
     We at his feet may fall!
   We'll join the everlasting song
     And crown him Lord of all.
   We'll join the everlasting song
     And crown him Lord of all.

Edward Perronet, 1726-1792, alt.   (LBW 328)

42   I Know that My Redeemer Lives!

1 I know that my Redeemer lives!
What comfort this sweet sentence gives!
He lives, he lives, who once was dead;
He lives, my everliving head!

2 He lives triumphant from the grave;
He lives eternally to save;
He lives exalted, throned above;
He lives to rule his Church in love.

3 He lives to grant me rich supply;
He lives to guide me with his eye;
He lives to comfort me when faint;
He lives to hear my soul's complaint.

4 He lives to silence all my fears;
He lives to wipe away my tears;
He lives to calm my troubled heart;
He lives all blessings to impart.

5 He lives to bless me with his love;
He lives to plead for me above;
He lives my hungry soul to feed;
He lives to help in time of need.

6 He lives, my kind, wise, heav'nly friend;
He lives and loves me to the end;
He lives, and while he lives, I'll sing;
He lives, my Prophet, Priest, and King!

7 He lives and grants me daily breath;
  He lives, and I shall conquer death;
  He lives my mansion to prepare;
  He lives to bring me safely there.

8 He lives, all glory to his name!
  He lives, my Savior, still the same;
  What joy this blest assurance gives:
  I know that my Redeemer lives!

Samuel Medley, 1738-1799, alt.   (LBW 352)

Almighty God, you give us the joy of celebrating our Lord's resurrection. Give us also the joys of life in your service, and bring us at last to the full joy of life eternal; through your Son, Jesus Christ our Lord, who lives and reigns with you and the Holy Spirit, one God, now and forever. Amen

43 Rock of Ages, Cleft for Me

1 Rock of Ages, cleft for me,
Let me hide myself in thee;
Let the water and the blood,
From thy riven side which flowed,
Be of sin the double cure:
Cleanse me from its guilt and pow'r.

2 Not the labors of my hands
Can fulfill thy law's demands;
Could my zeal no respite know,
Could my tears forever flow,
All for sin could not atone;
Thou must save, and thou alone.

3 Nothing in my hand I bring;
Simply to thy cross I cling.
Naked, come to thee for dress;
Helpless, look to thee for grace;
Foul, I to the fountain fly;
Wash me, Savior, or I die.

4 While I draw this fleeting breath,
When mine eyelids close in death,
When I soar to worlds unknown,
See thee on thy judgment throne,
Rock of Ages, cleft for me,
Let me hide myself in thee.

Augustus M. Toplady, 1740-1778 (LBW 327)

My Hope Is Built on Nothing Less 44

1 My hope is built on nothing less
Than Jesus' blood and righteousness;
No merit of my own I claim,
But wholly lean on Jesus' name.
On Christ, the solid rock, I stand;
All other ground is sinking sand.

2 When darkness veils his lovely face,
I rest on his unchanging grace;
In ev'ry high and stormy gale
My anchor holds within the veil.
On Christ, the solid rock, I stand;
All other ground is sinking sand.

3 His oath, his covenant, his blood
Sustain me in the raging flood;
When all supports are washed away,
He then is all my hope and stay.
On Christ, the solid rock, I stand;
All other ground is sinking sand.

4 When he shall come with trumpet sound,
Oh, may I then in him be found,
Clothed in his righteousness alone,
Redeemed to stand before the throne!
On Christ, the solid rock, I stand;
All other ground is sinking sand.

Edward Mote, 1787-1874, alt. (LBW 293)

45   Just as I Am, without One Plea

1 Just as I am, without one plea,
But that thy blood was shed for me,
And that thou bidd'st me come to thee,
O Lamb of God, I come, I come.

2 Just as I am, and waiting not
To rid my soul of one dark blot,
To thee, whose blood can cleanse each spot,
O Lamb of God, I come, I come.

3 Just as I am, though tossed about
With many a conflict, many a doubt,
Fightings and fears within, without,
O Lamb of God, I come, I come.

4 Just as I am, poor, wretched, blind;
Sight, riches, healing of the mind,
Yea, all I need, in thee to find,
O Lamb of God, I come, I come.

5 Just as I am, thou wilt receive,
Wilt welcome, pardon, cleanse, relieve;
Because thy promise I believe,
O Lamb of God, I come, I come.

6 Just as I am; thy love unknown
Has broken ev'ry barrier down;
Now to be thine, yea, thine alone,
O Lamb of God, I come, I come.

Charlotte Elliott, 1789-1871   (LBW 296)

I Lay My Sins on Jesus 46

1 I lay my sins on Jesus,
  The spotless Lamb of God;
He bears them all and frees us
  From the accursèd load.
I bring my guilt to Jesus
  To wash my crimson stains
Clean in his blood most precious
  Till not a spot remains.

2 I lay my wants on Jesus;
  All fullness dwells in him;
He heals all my diseases;
  My soul he does redeem.
I lay my griefs on Jesus,
  My burdens and my cares;
He from them all releases;
  He all my sorrows shares.

3 I rest my soul on Jesus,
  This weary soul of mine;
His right hand me embraces;
  I on his breast recline.
I love the name of Jesus,
  Immanuel, Christ, the Lord;
Like fragrance on the breezes
  His name abroad is poured.

Horatius Bonar, 1808-1889

(LBW 305)

1 Built on a rock the Church shall stand,
Even when steeples are falling;
Crumbled have spires in ev'ry land,
Bells still are chiming and calling–
Calling the young and old to rest,
Calling the souls of those distressed,
Longing for life everlasting.

2 Not in our temples made with hands
God, the Almighty, is dwelling;
High in the heav'ns his temple stands,
All earthly temples excelling.
Yet he who dwells in heav'n above
Deigns to abide with us in love,
Making our bodies his temple.

3 We are God's house of living stones,
Built for his own habitation;
He fills our hearts, his humble thrones,
Granting us life and salvation.
Were two or three to seek his face,
He in their midst would show his grace,
Blessings upon them bestowing.

4 Yet in this house, an earthly frame,
Jesus the children is blessing;
Hither we come to praise his name,
Faith in our Savior confessing.
Jesus to us his Spirit sent,
Making with us his covenant,
Granting his children the kingdom.

5 Through all the passing years, O Lord,
   Grant that, when church bells are ringing,
   Many may come to hear God's Word
   Where he this promise is bringing:
   I know my own, my own know me;
   You, not the world, my face shall see;
   My peace I leave with you. Amen

© Nikolai F. S. Grundvig, 1783-1872;
tr. Carl Doving, 1867-1937, adapt.   (LBW 365)

Blest Be the Tie That Binds   48

1   Blest be the tie that binds
       Our hearts in Christian love;
    The unity of heart and mind
       Is like to that above.

2   Before our Father's throne
       We pour our ardent prayers;
    Our fears, our hopes, our aims are one,
       Our comforts and our cares.

3   We share our mutual woes,
       Our mutual burdens bear,
    And often for each other flows
       The sympathizing tear.

4   From sorrow, toil, and pain,
       And sin we shall be free;
    And perfect love and friendship reign
       Through all eternity.

John Fawcett, 1740-1817, alt.   (LBW 370)

The Church's One Foundation

1 The Church's one foundation
    Is Jesus Christ, her Lord;
She is his new creation
    By water and the Word.
From heav'n he came and sought her
    To be his holy bride;
With his own blood he bought her,
    And for her life he died.

2 Elect from ev'ry nation,
    Yet one o'er all the earth;
Her charter of salvation:
    One Lord, one faith, one birth.
One holy name she blesses,
    Partakes one holy food,
And to one hope she presses
    With ev'ry grace endued.

3 Though with a scornful wonder
    This world sees her oppressed,
By schisms rent asunder,
    By heresies distressed,
Yet saints their watch are keeping;
    Their cry goes up: "How long?"
And soon the night of weeping
    Shall be the morn of song.

4 Through toil and tribulation
    And tumult of her war,
She waits the consummation
    Of peace forevermore;
Till with the vision glorious
    Her longing eyes are blest,
And the great Church victorious
    Shall be the Church at rest.

5 Yet she on earth has union
    With God, the Three in One,
And mystic sweet communion
    With those whose rest is won.
O blessèd heav'nly chorus!
    Lord, save us by your grace,
That we, like saints before us,
    May see you face to face.

Samuel J. Stone, 1839-1900   (LBW 369)

We remember with thanksgiving those who have loved and served you in your Church on earth, who now rest from their labors. Keep us in fellowship with all your saints, and bring us at last to the joy of your heavenly kingdom. Amen

50   Praise to the Lord, the Almighty

1 Praise to the Lord, the Almighty, the King
    of creation!
 O my soul, praise him, for he is your health
    and salvation!
    Let all who hear
    Now to his temple draw near,
    Joining in glad adoration!

2 Praise to the Lord, who o'er all things is wondrously
    reigning
 And, as on wings of an eagle, uplifting, sustaining.
    Have you not seen
    All that is needful has been
    Sent by his gracious ordaining?

3 Praise to the Lord, who will prosper your work
    and defend you;
 Surely his goodness and mercy shall daily
    attend you.
    Ponder anew
    What the Almighty can do
    If with his love he befriend you.

4 Praise to the Lord! Oh, let all that is in me
    adore him!
 All that has life and breath, come now with
    praises before him!
    Let the amen
    Sound from his people again.
    Gladly forever adore him!

Joachim Neander, 1650-1680;   (LBW 543)
tr. Catherine Winkworth, 1829-1878, alt.

Joyful, Joyful We Adore Thee 51

1 Joyful, joyful we adore thee,
   God of glory, Lord of love!
Hearts unfold like flow'rs before thee,
   Praising thee, their sun above.
Melt the clouds of sin and sadness,
   Drive the gloom of doubt away.
Giver of immortal gladness,
   Fill us with the light of day.

2 All thy works with joy surround thee,
   Earth and heav'n reflect thy rays,
Stars and angels sing around thee,
   Center of unbroken praise.
Field and forest, vale and mountain,
   Flow'ry meadow, flashing sea,
Chanting bird, and flowing fountain
   Call us to rejoice in thee.

3 Thou art giving and forgiving,
   Ever blessing, ever blest,
Wellspring of the joy of living,
   Ocean-depth of happy rest!
Thou our Father, Christ our brother,
   All who live in love are thine;
Teach us how to love each other,
   Lift us to the joy divine!

© Henry van Dyke, 1852-1933

(LBW 551)

 # Come, Thou Almighty King

1 Come, thou almighty King,
  Help us thy name to sing;
    Help us to praise;
  Father all-glorious,
  O'er all victorious,
  Come and reign over us,
    Ancient of Days.

2 Come, thou incarnate Word,
  Gird on thy mighty sword;
    Our prayer attend.
  Come and thy people bless,
  And give thy Word success,
  And let thy righteousness
    On us descend.

3 Come, holy Comforter,
  Thy sacred witness bear
    In this glad hour!
  Thou, who almighty art,
  Now rule in ev'ry heart,
  And ne'er from us depart,
    Spirit of pow'r.

4 To thee, great One in Three,
  Eternal praises be
    Hence evermore!
  Thy sov'reign majesty
  May we in glory see,
  And to eternity
    Love and adore.

Source unknown, c. 1757, alt.   (LBW 522)

Now Thank We All Our God 53

1   Now thank we all our God
With hearts and hands and voices,
    Who wondrous things has done,
In whom his world rejoices;
    Who, from our mothers' arms,
    Has blest us on our way
    With countless gifts of love,
    And still is ours today.

2   Oh, may this bounteous God
Through all our life be near us,
    With ever joyful hearts
And blessèd peace to cheer us,
    And keep us in his grace,
    And guide us when perplexed,
    And free us from all harm
    In this world and the next.

3   All praise and thanks to God
The Father now be given,
    The Son, and him who reigns
With them in highest heaven,
    The one eternal God,
    Whom earth and heav'n adore;
    For thus it was, is now,
    And shall be evermore.

Martin Rinkhart, 1586-1649;
tr. Catherine Winkworth, 1829-1878

(LBW 533)

 # O Savior, Precious Savior

1 O Savior, precious Savior,
    Whom yet unseen we love;
  O name of might and favor,
    All other names above:
  We worship thee; we bless thee;
    To thee alone we sing;
  We praise thee and confess thee,
    Our holy Lord and King.

2 O Bringer of salvation,
    Who wondrously hast wrought,
  Thyself the revelation
    Of love beyond our thought:
  We worship thee; we bless thee;
    To thee alone we sing;
  We praise thee and confess thee,
    Our gracious Lord and King.

3 In thee all fullness dwelleth,
    All grace and pow'r divine;
  The glory that excelleth,
    O Son of God, is thine.
  We worship thee; we bless thee;
    To thee alone we sing;
  We praise thee and confess thee,
    Our glorious Lord and King.

4 Oh, grant the consummation
    Of this our song above,

In endless adoration
  And everlasting love;
Then shall we praise and bless thee
  Where perfect praises ring,
And evermore confess thee,
  Our Savior and our King!

Frances R. Havergal, 1836-1879   (LBW 514)

Immortal, Invisible, God Only Wise   55

1 Immortal, invisible, God only wise,
  In light inaccessible hid from our eyes,
  Most blessèd, most glorious, the Ancient of Days,
  Almighty, victorious, thy great name we praise!

2 Unresting, unhasting, and silent as light,
  Nor wanting, nor wasting, thou rulest in might;
  Thy justice like mountains high soaring above
  Thy clouds which are fountains of goodness and
      love.

3 To all, life thou givest, to both great and small;
  In all life thou livest, the true life of all;
  We blossom and flourish like leaves on the tree,
  And wither and perish, but naught changeth thee.

4 Thou reignest in glory; thou dwellest in light;
  Thine angels adore thee, all veiling their sight;
  All laud we would render; oh, help us to see
  'Tis only the splendor of light hideth thee!

W. Chalmers Smith, 1824-1908, alt.   (LBW 526)

56   Jesus Shall Reign

1 Jesus shall reign where'er the sun
Does its successive journeys run;
His kingdom stretch from shore to shore,
Till moons shall wax and wane no more.

2 To him shall endless prayer be made,
And praises throng to crown his head;
His name like sweet perfume shall rise
With ev'ry morning sacrifice.

3 People and realms of ev'ry tongue
Dwell on his love with sweetest song;
And infant voices shall proclaim
Their early blessings on his name.

4 Blessings abound where'er he reigns:
The pris'ners leap to lose their chains,
The weary find eternal rest,
And all who suffer want are blest.

5 Let ev'ry creature rise and bring
Honors peculiar to our King;
Angels descend with songs again,
And earth repeat the loud amen.

Isaac Watts, 1674-1748, alt.   (LBW 530)

Beautiful Savior 57

1   Beautiful Savior,
      King of creation,
    Son of God and Son of Man!
      Truly I'd love thee,
      Truly I'd serve thee,
    Light of my soul, my joy, my crown.

2   Fair are the meadows,
      Fair are the woodlands,
    Robed in flow'rs of blooming spring;
      Jesus is fairer,
      Jesus is purer,
    He makes our sorrowing spirit sing.

3   Fair is the sunshine,
      Fair is the moonlight,
    Bright the sparkling stars on high;
      Jesus shines brighter,
      Jesus shines purer
    Than all the angels in the sky.

4   Beautiful Savior,
      Lord of the nations,
    Son of God and Son of Man!
      Glory and honor,
      Praise, adoration,
    Now and forevermore be thine!

Gesangbuch, Münster, 1677;   (LBW 518)
tr. Joseph A. Seiss, 1823-1904

1 O Lord my God, when I in awesome wonder
   Consider all the worlds* thy hand hath made,
I see the stars, I hear the rolling* thunder,
   Thy pow'r throughout the universe displayed;
Then sings my soul, my Savior God, to thee,
   How great thou art!
   How great thou art!
Then sings my soul, my Savior God, to thee,
   How great thou art!
   How great thou art!

2 When through the woods and forest glades I
     wander,
   I hear the birds sing sweetly in the trees;
When I look down from lofty mountain grandeur
   And hear the brook and feel the gentle breeze;
Then sings my soul, my Savior God, to thee,
   How great thou art!
   How great thou art!
Then sings my soul, my Savior God, to thee,
   How great thou art!
   How great thou art!

* Author's original words are "works" and "mighty."

3 But when I think that God, his Son not sparing,
   Sent him to die, I scarce can take it in,
That on the cross my burden gladly bearing
   He bled and died to take away my sin;
Then sings my soul, my Savior God, to thee,
   How great thou art!
   How great thou art!
Then sings my soul, my Savior God, to thee,
   How great thou art!
   How great thou art!

4 When Christ shall come, with shout of acclamation,
   And take me home, what joy shall fill my heart!
Then I shall bow in humble adoration
   And there proclaim, "My God, how great thou
      art!"
Then sings my soul, my Savior God, to thee,
   How great thou art!
   How great thou art!
Then sings my soul, my Savior God, to thee,
   How great thou art!
   How great thou art!

59 My God, How Wonderful Thou Art

1 My God, how wonderful thou art,
   Thy majesty how bright!
How beautiful thy mercy seat
   In depths of burning light!

2 How wonderful, how beautiful
   The sight of thee must be—
Thine endless wisdom, boundless pow'r,
   And awesome purity!

3 No earthly father loves like thee;
   No mother, e'er so mild,
Bears and forbears as thou hast done
   With me, thy sinful child.

4 Yet I may love thee too, O Lord,
   Almighty as thou art,
For thou hast stooped to ask of me
   The love of my poor heart.

5 My God, how wonderful thou art,
   Thou everlasting friend!
On thee I stay my trusting heart
   Till faith in vision end.

Frederick W. Faber, 1814-1863   (LBW 524)

60 For the Beauty of the Earth

1 For the beauty of the earth,
   For the beauty of the skies,
For the love which from our birth
   Over and around us lies:

Christ, our Lord, to you we raise
This our sacrifice of praise.

2 For the wonder of each hour
Of the day and of the night,
Hill and vale and tree and flow'r,
Sun and moon and stars of light:
Christ, our Lord, to you we raise
This our sacrifice of praise.

3 For the joy of ear and eye,
For the heart and mind's delight,
For the mystic harmony
Linking sense to sound and sight:
Christ, our Lord, to you we raise
This our sacrifice of praise.

4 For the joy of human love,
Brother, sister, parent, child,
Friends on earth and friends above;
For all gentle thoughts and mild:
Christ, our Lord, to you we raise
This our sacrifice of praise.

5 For yourself, best gift divine
To the world so freely giv'n;
Agent of God's grand design,
Peace on earth and joy in heav'n:
Christ, our Lord, to you we raise
This our sacrifice of praise.

Folliott S. Pierpoint, 1835-1917, alt.   (LBW 561)

1   This is my Father's world,
      And to my list'ning ears
   All nature sings, and round me rings
      The music of the spheres.
      This is my Father's world;
      I rest me in the thought
   Of rocks and trees, of skies and seas;
      His hand the wonders wrought.

2   This is my Father's world;
      The birds their carols raise;
   The morning light, the lily white,
      Declare their maker's praise.
      This is my Father's world;
      He shines in all that's fair.
   In the rustling grass I hear him pass;
      He speaks to me ev'rywhere.

3   This is my Father's world;
      Oh, let me not forget
   That, though the wrong seems oft so strong,
      God is the ruler yet.
      This is my Father's world;
      Why should my heart be sad?
   The Lord is king, let the heavens ring;
      God reigns, let the earth be glad!

Maltbie D. Babcock, 1858-1901   (LBW 554)

Faith of Our Fathers

62

1 Faith of our fathers, living still
   In spite of dungeon, fire, and sword.
   Oh, how our hearts beat high with joy
   Whene'er we hear that glorious word.
   Faith of our fathers, holy faith,
   We will be true to thee till death.

2 The martyrs, chained in prisons dark,
   Were still in heart and conscience free;
   And blest would be their children's fate
   If they, like them, should die for thee.
   Faith of our fathers, holy faith,
   We will be true to thee till death.

3 Faith of our fathers! We will love
   Both friend and foe in all our strife;
   Proclaim thee, too, as love knows how,
   By saving Word and faithful life.
   Faith of our fathers, holy faith,
   We will be true to thee till death.

Frederick W. Faber, 1814-1863, alt.   (LBW 500)

                                       # He Leadeth Me

1 He leadeth me: oh, blessed thought!
Oh, words with heav'nly comfort fraught!
Whate'er I do, where'er I be,
Still 'tis God's hand that leadeth me.
He leadeth me, he leadeth me,
By his own hand he leadeth me.
His faithful foll'wer I would be,
For by his hand he leadeth me.

2 Sometimes mid scenes of deepest gloom,
Sometimes where Eden's bowers bloom,
By waters calm, o'er troubled sea,
Still 'tis God's hand that leadeth me.
He leadeth me, he leadeth me,
By his own hand he leadeth me.
His faithful foll'wer I would be,
For by his hand he leadeth me.

3 Lord, I would clasp thy hand in mine,
Nor ever murmur nor repine;
Content, whatever lot I see,
Since 'tis my God that leadeth me.
He leadeth me, he leadeth me,
By his own hand he leadeth me.
His faithful foll'wer I would be,
For by his hand he leadeth me.

4 And when my task on earth is done,
When by thy grace the vict'ry's won,
E'en death's cold wave I will not flee,
Since God through Jordan leadeth me.
He leadeth me, he leadeth me,
By his own hand he leadeth me.
His faithful foll'wer I would be,
For by his hand he leadeth me.

Joseph H. Gilmore, 1834-1918, alt. (LBW 501)

O Master, Let Me Walk with You   64

1 O Master, let me walk with you
In lowly paths of service true;
Tell me your secret; help me bear
The strain of toil, the fret of care.

2 Help me the slow of heart to move
By some clear, winning word of love;
Teach me the wayward feet to stay,
And guide them in the homeward way.

3 Teach me your patience; share with me
A closer, dearer company,
In work that keeps faith sweet and strong,
In trust that triumphs over wrong,

4 In hope that sends a shining ray
Far down the future's broad'ning way,
In peace that only you can give;
With you, O Master, let me live.

Washington Gladden, 1836-1918 (LBW 492)

65 Dear Lord and Father of Mankind

1 Dear Lord and Father of mankind,
    Forgive our fev'rish ways;
Reclothe us in our rightful mind;
In purer lives thy service find,
    In deeper rev'rence, praise.

2 In simple trust like theirs who heard,
    Beside the Syrian sea,
The gracious calling of the Lord,
Let us, like them, without a word
    Rise up and follow thee.

3 Oh, Sabbath rest by Galilee,
    Oh, calm of hills above;
Where Jesus knelt to share with thee
The silence of eternity,
    Interpreted by love!

4 Drop thy still dews of quietness,
    Till all our strivings cease;
Take from our souls the strain and stress,
And let our ordered lives confess
    The beauty of thy peace.

5 Breathe through the heats of our desire
    Thy coolness and thy balm;
Let sense be dumb, let flesh retire;
Speak through the earthquake, wind, and fire,
    O still small voice of calm!

John G. Whittier, 1807-1892   (LBW 506)

Take My Life, that I May Be 66

1 Take my life, that I may be
Consecrated, Lord, to thee;
Take my moments and my days;
Let them flow in ceaseless praise.

2 Take my hands and let them move
At the impulse of thy love;
Take my feet and let them be
Swift and beautiful for thee.

3 Take my voice and let me sing
Always, only, for my King;
Take my lips and let them be
Filled with messages from thee.

4 Take my silver and my gold,
Not a mite would I withhold;
Take my intellect, and use
Ev'ry pow'r as thou shalt choose.

5 Take my will and make it thine;
It shall be no longer mine.
Take my heart, it is thine own;
It shall be thy royal throne.

6 Take my love; my Lord, I pour
At thy feet its treasure store;
Take myself, and I will be
Ever, only, all for thee.

Frances R. Havergal, 1836-1879, alt. (LBW 406)

67   Come, You Thankful People, Come

1 Come, you thankful people, come;
  Raise the song of harvest home.
  All is safely gathered in
  Ere the winter storms begin.
  God, our maker, does provide
  For our wants to be supplied.
  Come to God's own temple, come,
  Raise the song of harvest home.

2 All the world is God's own field,
  Fruit unto his praise to yield.
  Wheat and tares together sown,
  Unto joy or sorrow grown.
  First the blade, and then the ear,
  Then the full corn shall appear.
  Lord of harvest, grant that we
  Wholesome grain and pure may be.

3 For the Lord our God shall come
  And shall take his harvest home.
  From his field shall in that day
  All offenses purge away,
  Give his angels charge at last
  In the fire the tares to cast,
  But the fruitful ears to store
  In his garner evermore.

4 Even so, Lord, quickly come
To your final harvest home.
Gather all your people in,
Free from sorrow, free from sin,
There, forever purified,
In your garner to abide.
Come, with all your angels, come,
Raise the glorious harvest home!

Henry Alford, 1810-1871, alt.   (LBW 407)

The Lord is faithful in all his words
    and merciful in all his deeds.
The Lord upholds all those who fall;
    he lifts up those
    who are bowed down.
The eyes of all wait upon you, O Lord,
    and you give them their food
    in due season.
You open wide your hand
    and satisfy the needs
    of every living creature.
The Lord is righteous in all his ways
    and loving in all his works.

Psalm 145:14-18

1 Praise and thanksgiving,
  Father, we offer
  For all things living,
    Created good:
  Harvest of sown fields,
  Fruits of the orchard,
  Hay from the mown fields,
    Blossom and wood.

2 Bless, Lord, the labor
  We bring to serve you,
  That with our neighbor
    We may be fed.
  Sowing or tilling,
  We would work with you,
  Harvesting, milling
    For daily bread.

3 Father, providing
  Food for your children,
  By your wise guiding
    Teach us to share
  One with another,
  So that, rejoicing
  With us, all others
    May know your care.

4 Then will your blessing
Reach ev'ry people,
Freely confessing
    Your gracious hand.
Where all obey you,
No one will hunger;
In your love's sway you
    Nourish the land.

© Albert F. Bayly, b. 1901, alt.   (LBW 409)

Children of the Heavenly Father   69

1 Children of the heav'nly Father
Safely in his bosom gather;
Nestling bird or star in heaven
Such a refuge ne'er was given.

2 God his own doth tend and nourish,
In his holy courts they flourish.
From all evil things he spares them,
In his mighty arms he bears them.

3 Neither life nor death shall ever
From the Lord his children sever;
Unto them his grace he showeth,
And their sorrows all he knoweth.

4 Though he giveth or he taketh,
God his children ne'er forsaketh;
His the loving purpose solely
To preserve them pure and holy.

© Caroline V. Sandell Berg, 1832-1903;   (LBW 474)
tr. Ernst W. Olson, 1870-1958

     My Faith Looks Up to Thee

1 My faith looks up to thee,
Thou Lamb of Calvary,
  Savior divine!
Now hear me while I pray,
Take all my guilt away,
Oh, let me from this day
  Be wholly thine!

2 May thy rich grace impart
Strength to my fainting heart,
  My zeal inspire;
As thou hast died for me,
Oh, may my love to thee
Pure, warm, and changeless be,
  A living fire!

3 While life's dark maze I tread
And griefs around me spread,
  Be thou my guide;
Bid darkness turn to day,
Wipe sorrow's tears away,
Nor let me ever stray
  From thee aside.

4 When ends life's transient dream,
   When death's cold, sullen stream
      Shall o'er me roll;
   Blest Savior, then, in love
   Fear and distrust remove;
   Oh, bear me safe above,
      A ransomed soul!

Ray Palmer, 1808-1887   (LBW 479)

Amazing Grace   71

1 Amazing grace, how sweet the sound,
   That saved a wretch like me!
   I once was lost, but now am found;
   Was blind, but now I see.

2 'Twas grace that taught my heart to fear,
   And grace my fears relieved;
   How precious did that grace appear
   The hour I first believed!

3 Through many dangers, toils, and snares
   I have already come;
   'Tis grace has brought me safe thus far,
   And grace will lead me home.

4 The Lord has promised good to me;
   His Word my hope secures;
   He will my shield and portion be
   As long as life endures.

John Newton, 1725-1807   (LBW 448)

72 When I Survey the Wondrous Cross

1 When I survey the wondrous cross
On which the prince of glory died,
My richest gain I count but loss
And pour contempt on all my pride.

2 Forbid it, Lord, that I should boast
Save in the death of Christ, my God;
All the vain things that charm me most,
I sacrifice them to his blood.

3 See, from his head, his hands, his feet,
Sorrow and love flow mingled down.
Did e'er such love and sorrow meet,
Or thorns compose so rich a crown?

4 Were the whole realm of nature mine,
That were a tribute far too small;
Love so amazing, so divine,
Demands my soul, my life, my all!

Isaac Watts, 1674-1748   (LBW 482)

73 What Wondrous Love Is This

1 What wondrous love is this, O my soul,
     O my soul!
   What wondrous love is this, O my soul!
   What wondrous love is this
   That caused the Lord of bliss

To bear the dreadful curse for my soul,
    for my soul,
  To bear the dreadful curse for my soul?

2 When I was sinking down, sinking down,
    sinking down,
  When I was sinking down, sinking down,
  When I was sinking down
  Beneath God's righteous frown,
  Christ laid aside his crown for my soul,
    for my soul,
  Christ laid aside his crown for my soul.

3 To God and to the Lamb I will sing, I will sing;
  To God and to the Lamb I will sing;
  To God and to the Lamb,
  Who is the great I Am,
  While millions join the theme, I will sing,
    I will sing,
  While millions join the theme, I will sing.

4 And when from death I'm free, I'll sing on,
    I'll sing on;
  And when from death I'm free, I'll sing on;
  And when from death I'm free,
  I'll sing his love for me,
  And through eternity I'll sing on, I'll sing on;
    And through eternity I'll sing on.

American folk hymn, alt.   (LBW 385)

      # I Love to Tell the Story

1 I love to tell the story
   Of unseen things above,
Of Jesus and his glory,
   Of Jesus and his love.
I love to tell the story,
   Because I know it's true;
It satisfies my longings
   As nothing else would do.
I love to tell the story;
I'll sing this theme in glory
And tell the old, old story
   Of Jesus and his love.

2 I love to tell the story:
   How pleasant to repeat
What seems, each time I tell it,
   More wonderfully sweet!
I love to tell the story,
   For some have never heard
The message of salvation
   From God's own holy Word.
I love to tell the story;
I'll sing this theme in glory
And tell the old, old story
   Of Jesus and his love.

3 I love to tell the story,
    For those who know it best
Seem hungering and thirsting
    To hear it like the rest.
And when, in scenes of glory,
    I sing the new, new song,
I'll sing the old, old story
    That I have loved so long.
I love to tell the story;
I'll sing this theme in glory
And tell the old, old story
    Of Jesus and his love.

Katherine Hankey, 1834-1911   (LBW 390)

O God, increase the faith and energy of your Church
to desire and work for the salvation of all people,
that they might be freed from sin and that hope be
renewed in many hearts, to the increase of the kingdom of your Son, Jesus Christ our Lord. Amen

75   Lift High the Cross

Lift high the cross, the love of Christ proclaim
Till all the world adore his sacred name.

1 Come, Christians, follow where our captain trod,
Our king victorious, Christ, the Son of God.
Lift high the cross, the love of Christ proclaim
Till all the world adore his sacred name.

2 Led on their way by this triumphant sign,
The hosts of God in conqu'ring ranks combine.
Lift high the cross, the love of Christ proclaim
Till all the world adore his sacred name.

3 All newborn soldiers of the Crucified
Bear on their brows the seal of him who died.
Lift high the cross, the love of Christ proclaim
Till all the world adore his sacred name.

4 O Lord, once lifted on the glorious tree,
As thou hast promised, draw us all to thee.
Lift high the cross, the love of Christ proclaim
Till all the world adore his sacred name.

5 So shall our song of triumph ever be:
Praise to the Crucified for victory!
Lift high the cross, the love of Christ proclaim
Till all the world adore his sacred name.

(LBW 377)

1 What a friend we have in Jesus,
   All our sins and griefs to bear!
What a privilege to carry
   Ev'rything to God in prayer!
Oh, what peace we often forfeit;
   Oh, what needless pain we bear—
All because we do not carry
   Ev'rything to God in prayer!

2 Have we trials and temptations?
   Is there trouble anywhere?
We should never be discouraged—
   Take it to the Lord in prayer.
Can we find a friend so faithful
   Who will all our sorrows share?
Jesus knows our ev'ry weakness—
   Take it to the Lord in prayer.

3 Are we weak and heavy-laden,
   Cumbered with a load of care?
Precious Savior, still our refuge—
   Take it to the Lord in prayer.
Do your friends despise, forsake you?
   Take it to the Lord in prayer.
In his arms he'll take and shield you;
   You will find a solace there.

Joseph Scriven, 1820-1886   (LBW 439)

TOPICAL INDEX

INDEX OF FIRST LINES*

  * Accompaniments to these hymns may be found in **Lutheran Book of Worship.**

** Refers to hymn number in **Lutheran Book of Worship.**